# WHEN THE WORLD WAS BITTEN BY CORONA

## MY LOCKDOWN POEMS

SIDHARTH P K

Made with ♥ on the Notion Press Platform
www.notionpress.com

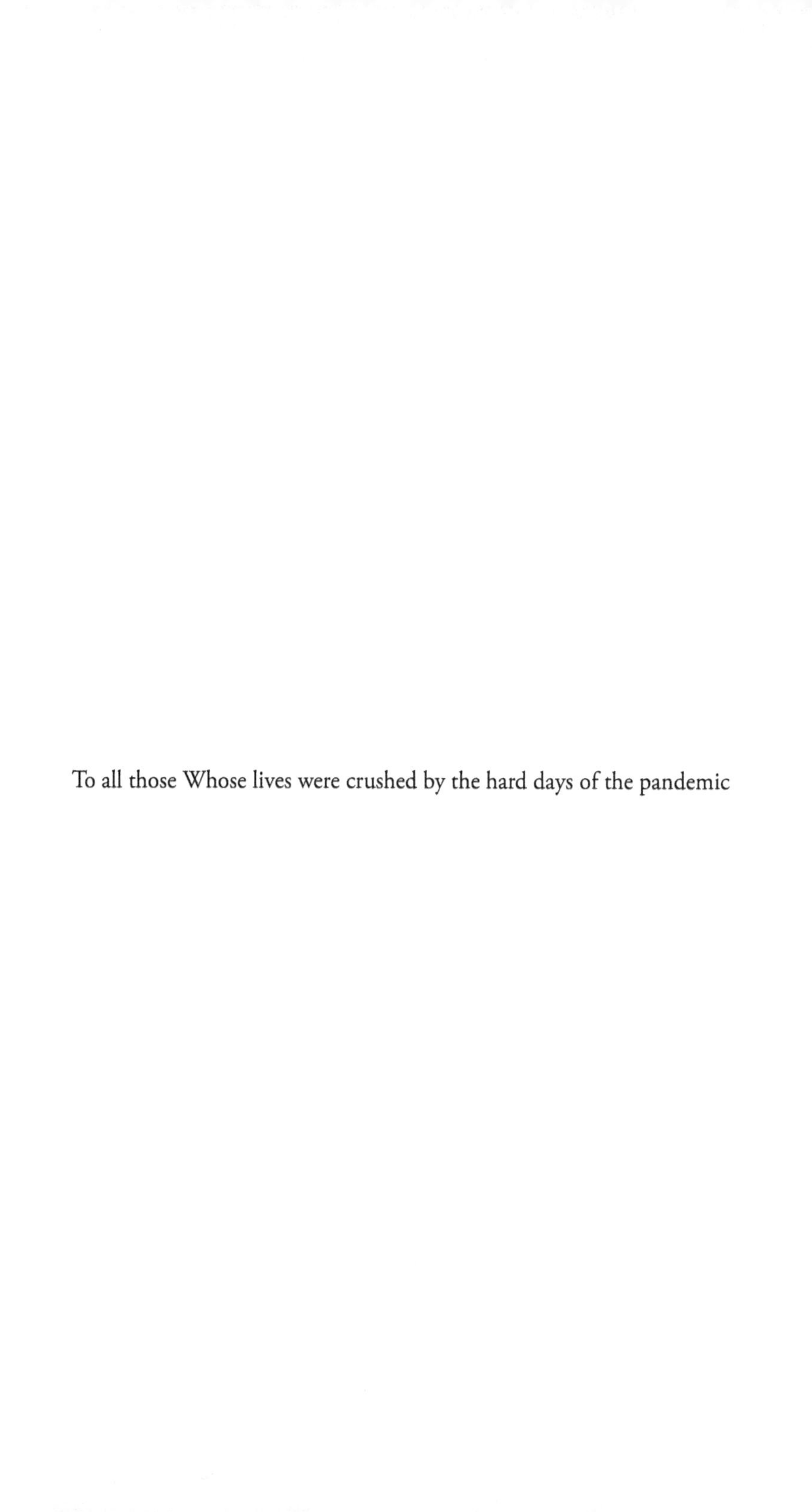

To all those Whose lives were crushed by the hard days of the pandemic

# Contents

# Foreword

The poems in this collection opines the notions of love, beauty and truth. The poems are written in a timeless sphere and it charms the beauty of verse. It carries the depth of meaning. The poet captures love , natural settings, uses rich imagery to underline the poems. The verses brings our attention the emotion of love even during man's fight against the corona virus . The poems of this collection is attack on the struggling pandemic times. The poet uses various poetic methods to highlight his creations.

# Preface

I'm glad and happy ,proud to state that, the lockdown days of mine has neér gone into vain. I used my lockdown times, to pen poems to quench my thirst for literature. I glad to present my new collection to my readers to find a solace in the time of the great pandemic.

Sidharth P k

Kochi.

# Acknowledgements

I take the chance to convey my heartfelt gratitude to my mother, in helping me with editing and proof reading my new collection. My younger brother is also an inspiration for me. Last but not the least , I thank all my well wishers in shaping this creation of mine. Thank you all.

Sidharth P.k

# 1. Oh Beautiful Girl

*My young girl, my heart moves*
*From fire to cold*
*And colder will be your kiss*
*Within my soul, yet extinguished*
*The flames of love, the blaze*
*Has let off it's glow*
*The dying light of love*
*Soon be losing it's beauty.*
*Beauty will last for long,*
*The bond between us is gone*
*My vows are all broken*
*Secrets we kept in our heart's chambers*
*Are enclosed forever*
*Silence is your language*
*And now mine too*
*Your absence is like a blow to me.*

# 2. Ode To a Young Quaker

*Oh love, wrap me in your*
*Blanket of love*
*You play with the light*
*Of the moon.*
*Thy face softens like snow,*
*The cascade that bloom*
*Like a earthly flower*
*I wish to hold thy heart.*
*The glory and light of universe,*
*Kindles, yet no torch can behold*
*In the depths of my soul,*
*I can see your presence.*
*The moon wrapped in the blanket,*
*Of the eternal night*
*I want to die with you*
*Make a wish nor stay with me.*

# 3. Farewell I Sign

*No torch can kindle the flames,*
*Of mortal love and pain*
*Adieu, the very word like a knell*
*Blown by time and destiny.*
*The night rhymes a verse,*
*My spirit moves in vain*
*And sink in despair*
*Love painted in blood.*
*I sing deep in my heart,*
*Tear drops of parting love*
*Will we two meet again?*
*In a another world.*

# 4. Ode on Evening

*The bright moonlit skies,*
*With the brilliant stars*
*Crafts a constellation of the night*
*Gently unfurls the coy in her eyes.*
*The night sings the evening's lore,*
*Faint light from the Heaven's glory*
*There's music in the breeze blown by*
*Silence in her heart's core.*
*The moon unfolds the beauty,*
*Of the world and the magic*
*In you I find*
*But the day will come to soon.*

# 5. I Don't know you, But still I love

*The blue star shivers and overshadow*
*The dark skies of mystery*
*Her eyes of beauty carved*
*By the eternity of love*
*Her speech kissed my heart,*
*Tears left me motionless.*

# 6. Once in a Blue Moon

*Once in a blue moon,*
*We came to know eachother*
*Our wishes stood in the blood*
*Wrap me in the light of the universe*
*The stars mingle with the universe*
*Your eyes meet with mine.*
*The clouds hides you in vain,*
*My spirit goes into despair*
*Woes all are*
*The world will neér see you again*
*And my soul is not much pure*
*Nor the innocence in the heart.*
*Light shares wisdom in solitude,*
*Despairing and hour by hour pass by*
*Night echoes the spirit of love*
*There is motion in the waters,*
*Stars shines in vain*
*A ray of hope still I carry.*

# 7. To My Fair Love

*The evening star shoots up in the horizon,*
*Night singing a song*
*Moon bleeds in blood*
*Far off the distance*
*I hear the song of a girl*
*To which I dance.*
*Her eyes like the impeccable marble,*
*The cloud shed tears*
*Of vain and solitude*
*I crave for her presence*
*Into darkness, did she vanish*
*Leaving no clue or trace.*
*She is like a beautiful poem,*
*A poem written in blood*
*The flow of her song*
*Takes me into her*
*Magical world*
*Of love and hope.*

# 8. The Evening

*The sun oér the medieterran sea,*
*The wind kissing the shore*
*Moon came out from the blanket*
*Of the starry azure.*
*Come let's go and touch the star,*
*The eternal night overshadows*
*The world of mystery*
*Let me sleep on the lap of time.*
*The dawn will arrive,*
*Darkness to be erazed off*
*A new sunshine in our lives*
*Will blossom.*

# 9. Epitaph To Femi

*O girl, I want to wrap you*
*Like little infants do*
*To heave upon thy good breast*
*Toss you into the inexorable air.*
*Your eyes like small pebbles,*
*Of the solitary ocean*
*I still love you without feeling*
*Your presence.*
*The worm and canker*
*Upon the yellow leaf*
*Shattered my dreams of you*
*The pledge is broken.*

# 10. Remember Me Not

*Remember me not,*
*When I'm gone into mystery*
*For my soul is not fair*
*Fair as the sunlight*
*And warm as the moon.*
*Don't weep for me,*
*In some sad tombs*
*For I will not be there*
*For I don't sleep there*
*Cease to cry for me.*
*Close your eyes, my girl*
*I will disappear into darkness*
*Into the silence*
*Into the mystery*
*And I will neér hear your voice.*

# 11. I Looked into her Eyes

*I looked into her eyes and saw*
*The wonders of this world*
*Her eyes crafted by the destiny*
*And time.*
*I peeped into her heart*
*I saw a young girl's love,*
*And the beat, swell and heave*
*Like a small infant.*
*There I can see an infant,*
*Weaving upon your good bosom*
*She blushed like the dawn*
*So eloquent to spy upon.*

# 12. To Dona

*The sun is low and descending down,*
*The waters are gushing fast*
*Night wind kisses the tree*
*She is beautiful like the starry fair*
*Her eyes meet the crystalline twilight.*
*My tears are for thee,*
*Oh those ponderous tombs*
*Where last is the wish of love*
*Can snatch away in time's eternal gloom*
*And beauty cannot but be perish.*
*Death will smile at thee,*
*The doom will exceed life*
*I love thee for sure*
*What is to be remembered is love*
*Pure passion.*

# 13. Let Fair be your Hue

*The bright and silent moon,*
*Starlit skies revolves in the western*
*Hemphiser and the sleepy shore*
*Let fair be your hue.*
*I painted verses for thee,*
*Silence is the language of our love*
*I can see the destiny in thy eyes*
*Let fair be your hue.*
*The moon is still,*
*Desires within my spirit sinks*
*My heart cuts a channel to your cordon*
*Let fair be your hue.*
*I journey into the night,*
*Of mystery and darker the destiny*
*I pause to retain that thou no more, but*
*Let fair be your hue.*

# 14. Why The Night Hides you?

*Why the night hides you, in vain*
*The world swalloed you into mystery*
*You are hidden behind the shadows*
*Of the darkness*
*Your love is like frozen*
*Losing it's tenderness.*
*My heart pause to beat,*
*I lost you into the eternal night*
*My world only you understood*
*We together build our dreams*
*But dreams that never came true*
*And the image fades.*
*Our last days of togetherness,*
*Have it's touch upon my soul*
*The stars of heaven mingle*
*With my spirit and they*
*Speaks to me of you*
*Remember me, my young love.*

# 15. Hymn To a Young Girl

*The sun is low,*
*The skies are clear*
*Birds are humming*
*Your eyes of compassion*
*Like the blue sky*
*The earliest flowers of beauty*
*Can don an hat for you,*
*I gift you.*
*I want to embrace you,*
*Into the softness of my arms*
*Take you into silence*
*To hold your young heart*
*Till it's last beat*
*I can't stop loving you,*
*Oh girl of mystery.*
*The sun will go down,*
*Into the valley*
*And moon comes out*
*Weeping in pain*
*The pain of love*
*I want to expire with you*
*Into the pages of tomorrow,*
*To leave behind a mark of love.*
*The night consumes you,*

*Into the airy mystery*
*Let the blanket*
*Of love spread it's velvet*
*I hope to be with you*
*I'm only a poet*
*By destiny.*

# 16. I welcome The Night

*The stars lit up the beauty*
*Of it's gentle constellation*
*The torch and it's flame*
*Consume the world.*
*The blue star of western sky,*
*Dazzles in joy*
*Shows the strength of love,*
*Camphor fire bright in my camp.*
*The night like a young girl,*
*Whispers into my small ears*
*I see a march of shadows*
*And captures with my vision.*

# 17. On The Love to a Young Lady

*She captured my bleak vision,*
*Like the eptiome of care*
*The moon will weep in silence,*
*And admire you with reverence.*
*Thy eyes twinkle like the blue star,*
*The waters are flowing like blood*
*Clasp together into the beauty*
*And silence of love.*

# 18. My Heart Moves into Silence

*The brilliant stars in Heaven's outdoor,*
*Plays with the light of universe*
*The exultant moon peeps out*
*Behind the dark clouds.*
*I cry in the absence of thee,*
*I feel a shudder coming to me*
*Lowering the storm*
*Expire in vain.*

# 19. The Last Vow of Love

*My blood loses it's fire,*
*My life even in conquering pain*
*Your kiss left an delicate mark*
*Upon my dark soul.*
*I made a vow to you,*
*And that vow is now broken*
*By the fading light of the universe*
*We severed forever.*
*My heart roars in pain,*
*My soul is no longer pure*
*The dying flames of the torch*
*Extinguished forever.*

# 20. She Captured My Imagination

*Her eyes stood still,*
*Like the stars of eternity*
*Wrapped in the mist of love*
*Conquers my crumbling heart.*
*She is like a poem wriiten*
*She is like a picture painted in hue*
*She shines like the moon,*
*Of the starry skies.*
*Oh blood, and love for the night,*
*My love, I will soon come to thee*
*Even miles to travel,*
*I won't be far from you.*

# The End